I AM [NOT] KANYE WEST

Natasha Brown

TEAM
ANGE
LICA

Published March 2020 by Team Angelica Publishing,
an imprint of Angelica Entertainments Ltd

Team Angelica Publishing
51 Coningham Road
Shepherds Bush
London W12 8BS

TEAM
ANGELICA

www.teamangelica.com

A CIP catalogue record for this book is available from
the British Library

ISBN 978-1-9163561-0-8

Cover photograph by Holly Revell

Creative team

Performed and written by Natasha Brown
Dramaturgy by John R Gordon
Produced by Natasha Brown and Sculptress Theatre
Director: Abigail Sewell
Lighting Designer: Martha Godfrey
Sound Designer: Mwen
Stage Manager: Shereen Hamilton

I Am [Not] Kanye West was performed at The Bunker Theatre, 2nd – 7th March 2020, as part of the Power x Resistance Takeover. An earlier version, titled *Everything I Am*, was showcased at Camden People's Theatre in October 2018.

Natasha Brown is an actor, writer, theatre-maker and facilitator based in London. Her work interrogates power, identity and community. She is part of the Soho Writers' Lab and the Bush Theatre's Emerging Writers' Group. Natasha trained at The BRIT School and National Youth Theatre. She has a BA and Masters in Drama from the University of Kent and also studied at the University of California, Berkeley. *I Am [Not] Kanye West* is her debut play.

Abigail Sewell is a London-based director, facilitator and graduate of English Literature. She has trained on Young Vic's Intro to Directing, Springboard and Dramaturgy programmes, and Ovalhouse's Young Associate Artist traineeship.

As director, credits include: *Dance Nation*, ArtsEd; *PYNEAPPLE*, Bunker Theatre; *The Lost Ones*, Ovalhouse; *Never Forget*, Tristan Bates Theatre and *Heard*, Camden People's Theatre.

As assistant director, credits include: *Merchant of Venice*, Royal Shakespeare Company tour, dir. Robin Belfield; *Pah-La*, Royal Court Theatre, dir. Debbie Hannan; *Rosenbaum's Rescue*, Park Theatre, dir. Kate Fahy; *Things of Dry Hours*, Young Vic, dir. Debbie Hannan; *and Random Selfies*, Ovalhouse, dir. Owen Calvert-Lyons.

Sculptress Theatre is a theatre company that creates and produces new and exciting with creatives of colour, consisting of Alisha Artry and Germma Orleans-Thompson. Previous work includes: *Blue Beneath My Skin* (part of the This Is Black festival at The Bunker Theatre) and *Dark and Lovely* at the Rose Theatre Kingston. They were part of Creative Youth's Creative Talent Programme 2018/2019 and are recipients of a Stage One Producer's bursary.

Thank you to:

Stella Ajayi, Chrissy Angus, Alice Barraclough, Rikki Beadle-Blair, Perpetual Brade, Daisy Cooper, Charlotte Duff, Matthew Dwyer, John R Gordon, Kelly Green, Yasmin Hafesji, Christopher Haydon, Siobhan James-Elliot, Sophie Latham, Lynette Linton, Brian Logan, Lauren McLeggen, Lara Olusola, Holly Revell, Clare Slater, Courteleigh Smith, Holly Thompson, Camden People's Theatre, Donmar Warehouse, Shoreditch Town Hall and, of course, my incredibly patient family who have suffered through me reading aloud every draft of this script in my room.

THE BUNKER

LOTTERY FUNDED

Supported using public funding by
**ARTS COUNCIL
ENGLAND**

To my mum and dad

Natasha Brown

I AM [NOT] KANYE WEST

(Tash plays all the characters)

I'm in my Aunty Patsy's hair salon. My best friend, Victoria, is doing my hair because tomorrow I'm starting university and I need to look good.

Tash: I want you to make me look like a cross between Michelle Obama and Janelle Monáe. You know, respected yet rebellious. Dependable but fun. Straight but queer.

Victoria: Why do you say shit like this all the time, Tash? It's weird.

Tash: I'm carving out a fresh identity for myself, Victoria. I'm about to start a new chapter of my life. University is where you meet extraordinary people and learn extraordinary things. You wouldn't understand.

Victoria: Okay, well, how about I give you an extraordinary new haircut and shave it all off?

Tash: Alright! Sorry. I'm just excited, okay? I really think this might be the making of me. A place where I can finally transcend my multiple sites of oppression.

Victoria: *(Kisses teeth)* Oh, not all this again. 'I'm Black, I'm working class, I'm a woman.' We get it. I get it. I am those things too.

Tash: Yeah, but I'm also queer, Victoria. There are levels. And I can't ever get into it without you all rolling your eyes.

Victoria: Whatever. Shall I straighten your hair or are GHDs still a product of White Supremacy?

Tash: Er, they are indeed! But, yeah, you can. Just touch up the edges a bit.

This hair salon. An oasis for Black women. It's where you can get your hair done, get questionable relationship advice, and the best gossip all at once. But don't expect a quick service. Minimum time spent at *Grow Ur Fro*? 4 hours.

Victoria and I had to help out here every Saturday when we were younger. To give us a 'sense of responsibility'. *Unpaid* responsibility. But we never minded, coz there isn't any place we'd rather be. You see, this is more than just hair and beauty. This is a congregation – a chorus of voices from across the Caribbean. A space where a side eye, kissing of the teeth and a 'chah' is enough for everyone to understand exactly how you feel.

And everyone is always here! Aunties who aren't your aunties, cousins you didn't know you had, the next door neighbour, the Chinese manicurists, the Yardie you can't understand. *Everyone*. The place always smells like Morley's, some game show is always muted on the TV and Vybz

Kartel's homophobic lyrics are always on the radio. *(Looks uncomfortable)* I know, I should say something but... The beat is just so good. Anyway, I'm off to uni, so it doesn't matter.

While I was filling out my UCAS application, Victoria decided to get a job instead.

Victoria: I don't need a degree to validate me. Or 40k of debt.

So now she works at Pet Paradise selling insurance for small mammals. She started off with tarantulas but she's worked her way up to the Hamster Division. *(Laughs)*

Victoria: Laugh all you want, Tash, but remind me what you're studying again?

Tash: Drama.

You think 'coming out' to my Jamaican parents was hard — try telling them you're studying drama at uni.

Victoria still helps my Aunty out every now and then. My Aunty needs all the help she can get since nowadays she only does her favourite client's hair. Once, there were 6 people waiting to get their hair done and my Aunty just sat in her chair staring them in the face. *(Tash stares, unbothered)* If you've ever been to any establishment run by a Jamaican, you'll know the look. *(Tash stares, unbothered)* We pride ourselves on our customer service.

Aunty: Mmm mmm. Nasty, dutty peopledem out dere sah. Wid dem nasty, dutty hair. Me nah touch it. Me nah touch it! No sah. Unlike Carole. Carole is my friend so me truss her. Me know say she clean. Lawd a mercy! Chah. *(Kisses teeth)*

My Aunty can be very stuck in her ways. Everyone here sort of is. It's kind of lovely, but...

Put your hands up if you belong to a group that is marginalised? Hands up if you're from two groups? Three? More than three? Alright, show offs.

Victoria: Here we go with the Oppression Olympics, Tash.

Tash: Victoria! I've told you, it's a very real thing.

Being a Black, queer woman (shut up, Victoria) can be tricky. You're always a bit on edge. The very people who you expect to understand you, often don't. The marginalised marginalise.

Aunty Patsy calls my Dr Martens my 'lesbian boots' which the salon thinks is hilarious, Victoria laughs at me the moment I mention trigger warnings, and my parents think I just want my life to be more complicated than it already is.

I guess that's why I can't wait to get to uni. My kind of people are there. People who get it. Who are clued up. I won't have to explain myself. And, most importantly, my various identities won't be everything I am. At uni I can just be myself – figure out what that even means – and breathe. *(Deep breath.)* And join loads of societies! The French Society because you get a funded trip to Paris. The Hot Chocolate Society because I am a hot chocolate connoisseur. The When Beyonce Does That *(Tongue gesture)* in the 'Crazy in Love' Music Video Appreciation Society... for reasons... I just can't wait!

Tash: Thanks for doing my hair, babe. Bye Aunty Patsy.

Aunty Patsy: You muss remember fe eat. Don't be coming back here lookin' all mawga like Jackie's pickneydem.

Tash: Yes, Aunty.

*

5

Goodbye East London!

*

Hello 1960s university just outside the M25!

I'm at Freshers' Fayre, hovering near the Cheese Society's free samples, when this white guy approaches.

James: Ha. Do you have a cheese addiction too?

Tash: Ha. No.

James: Let me guess. First year? I remember those days. Try not to get Freshers' Flu. Ha!

Tash: Ha!

This guy has never spoken to a Black woman before. You know when you just know.

Tash: You've never spoken to a Black woman before, have you?

James: Christ! Of course I have. There's Abiola in the canteen, Shanice in admin, and, um, er. God, am I that awkward?

Tash: Yep. Well, I'm going to make my way over to the LGBTQ stall. See ya!

James: Oh. Are you...? You know... LGBTQ?

Tash: Am I LGBTQ? Yeah, all of them.

James: Ha! Really? But, like, are you?

Tash: I'm bisexual. I'm pansexual. Bi - No. Pan. No. Both. *(Deep breath)* I'm part of the queer community.

James: Brilliant. I'm James. Student Union President.

Tash: I'm Tash.

James: Vice President elections are coming up. Are you interested in politics at all?

Tash: Well, I look at Twitter a lot.

James: Epic. Would you meet me in my office tomorrow? Around 3pm? There's something I'd love to discuss with you.

James is about 6', with blonde, floppy hair. Has that generic, attractive white boy, young Jude Law look about him. I do some research. Doing an MA in politics. A self-proclaimed Centrist. Angling for a career in Westminster. Can't accept that he didn't get into Oxbridge. Wears his baseball cap backwards to show he's a man of the people. Probably fist-bumps with his 'bros'.

*

Tash: James, this isn't an office, it's a cupboard.

James: It's the cuts. The union's in a bad place financially and relevance-wise. Not helped by the Vice President stepping down. Drama in his Twitter timeline. Why people don't erase old tweets, I'll never understand. Anyway, he was pale, stale and male. And there can't be two of us! What we're looking for now, Tash, is someone relevant, who's really got a diverse life experience.

Tash: A diverse life experience?

James: Yeah. Black. A woman. LGBTQ... State school?

Tash: Yeah.

James: Working class?

Tash: Yeah.

James: Immigrant parents?

Tash: One of them.

James: Religious?

Tash: Sometimes.

James: Tell me to check my privilege but I think your intersections could really help us out. I need a vice president, a second in command, to join me in realising my vision for a diverse and inclusive campus, and you're top trumps.

Tash: You don't know anything about me.

James: Let's take a look at your potential competitors. First up there's Beth. Surprisingly good banter for a vegan environmentalist. Got disabilities. At this point you're thinking – perfect. Only it's *invisible* disabilities – so someone created a Twitter thread condemning her right to represent the community. It went viral and she's been quiet since. Then there's Ryan. He's from Up North and grew up in a single parent household, which people love. I, personally, thought that was a bit done but – scandal, back in the day he got a scholarship to a private school, so now there's a big debate as to whether he actually is working class.

Tash: This sounds complicated.

James: Oh, it is. This place is incredibly tribal. And vicious. Obviously, I don't mean 'tribal' in a sort of... Afri... gosh. No. You won't tweet that, will you? What I need is someone with a clean record, a fresh face to cut through the noise.

Tash: Right. To be honest, I just wanted to study some Brecht and tucker green, join some societies, maybe have sex. I think you're being dramatic about tribalism. The uni handbook says that everyone's identities are acknowledged and respected. We all get it.

James: God, you are a Fresher. Yes, everyone's 'woke', attending protests together, checking their privileges, staying in their lane, monitoring their micro-aggressions and unconscious biases, but people still have their

9

conscious biases. Everyone's fighting their corner. This *is* a place where you can be yourself. You just have to perform yourself too.

Tash: Perform myself?

James: Let's say you ran, okay? You'd have to change this. *(Gestures to her face)* This happy go lucky thing. We're angry here.

Tash: This is too much now. *(Starts to back away.)*

James: There's something about you. Something extraordinary, waiting to come out. Why do I get the feeling you're often misunderstood? Not appreciated? Not listened to?

Tash: No one really listens to me at the salon when I try to tell them about...

James: And how does that make you feel?

Tash: Frustrated. Alone.

James: I get lonely too. That's why it's so important to me to make a difference. To feel part of something. A community. This might be your moment. You and me fighting for change, together.

Tash: What change? What am I fighting? What am I supposed to say?

James: There's only one way to win. Make as much noise as possible. Call things out. Go for the jugular. Slavery, empire, white guilt, post-colonial...stuff. Make them feel like a vote for you is a pat on the back for them. 'Look at me, I'm not racist, I'm not homophobic, I'm not sexist. I voted for Tash.'

Tash: *(Frowning)* I'm not really a public speaker.

James: *(Pause)* If stage fright is what you're worried about then I've got just the thing. *(Pulls out Kanye West glasses)* Was planning to wear these to a fancy dress party but got called out for cultural appropriation. You a fan of Kanye West?

Tash: What? Yeah. Not really. I used to be, but... It's complicated.

James: Oh, is he cancelled now? Look, say what you want about the guy, he knows how to get attention. He speaks his mind, and people listen to him. Why don't you put these on every time you'd like people to listen to you?

Tash: *(Takes the glasses)* First of all, this isn't 2007. Second of all, I don't think they'll suit me.

James: Go on, try them on. For fun.

Tash: *(Hesitates, laughs nervously)* This is so weird.

Tash puts the glasses on. Everything becomes surreal.

Tash: I am Picasso! I am Basquiat! I am Shakespeare in the flesh! I'm a genius! The Louis Vuitton Don himself. What is my wife talented at? She's talented at being beautiful. George Bush doesn't care about Black people!

11

Tash takes the glasses off.

Tash: What. The. Fuck. What is this thing?

James: That was perfect. Come on, Tash! Speak up for the
left behind. Be listened to at last. And come and sit next
to me at the Student Senate.

Tash: *(Considers it)* No.

And I leave.

*

What the heck was that about?

*

Three days later and I get an invite to a private Lesbian
group on Facebook. This was the intel I've been gagging for.
I mean, obviously, I feel a bit weird because I'm not a
lesbian but... just let me have nice things!

I'm glad it's private as well - I don't need everyone at home
spying. I only want them to know what I tell them. When I

was 15, Aunty Patsy got Facebook and added me as a friend (why do they do this?). I *had* to accept otherwise there'd be non-stop questioning – 'a what is it ya a do on Facebook that you nah want me fe see?' I immediately blocked her from seeing any of my photos, statuses, likes, events. To this day, she thinks all I've ever said on Facebook is, 'Just received my GCSE results and thrilled to announce that I got 7 A*'s and 5 A's. Couldn't have done it without God, my family and friends.' I didn't get those grades.

Anyway, this Facebook group. I just want to lurk. I stalk a bunch of profiles – everyone's here! Baby queers, seasoned pros, butch, femme, stem, lipstick, chapstick, boi *(Inhales)* stone butch, soft butch, bambi, Alpha, Gold Star. Lesbian utopia!

I get a notification – a message from this white girl.

'Nice to see you in the group. I'm Chloe.' A potential friend. An actual queer friend. I've never had one before. I click on her profile, have a look at her picture – pink hair, septum piercing, defiant eyes. I click next (she really should update her privacy settings) – blue hair, tongue piercing, defiant eyes. She has nice eyes.

I don't know how to reply so I just don't. She asks if I want to go clubbing with her. To the queer night in town. Brilliant!

I hate clubbing. I don't really get what it is. My first experience at the campus nightclub, Nirvana, ended with a guy asking me whether I was new money or old money. I said 'no money, bitch.' I didn't say bitch.

But Chloe says this will be different. This club night is intimate, edgy, plays the best RnB and Hip Hop from the early Noughties and everyone's really cool. I can't wait.

*

The club is in this warehouse in the part of town people keep calling 'Our Shoreditch.' People who aren't from London. I spot Chloe waiting outside. Shit, she looks good. I didn't get the all-black memo. Why am I wearing this rainbow skirt?!

I say hi and awkwardly go to shake her hand. She looks at it and laughs. I don't.

She goes up to the person at the door, says 'Bigfoot' and we're in. The doors open and I'm hit with the smell of sweat and anticipation. Quick scan of the room. Everyone's got an undercut, a feather, anchor or arrow tattoo and Dr Martens for days. Nod to the Black girl in the corner, solidarity smile to the South Asian girl on the dancefloor. We are the only ones who aren't white. But that's okay. Chloe's right about the music, it is good.

We head straight to the bar.

'So,' she says

'So,' I say

Chloe: So, what do you think?

Tash: Yeah, this is a cool place.

Tash: So... *(To herself)* Think of something queer to say, think of something queer to say. *(To Chloe)* So... favourite character on *Sugar Rush*?'

'So,' she says, 'given that we're living in a time in which the achievements of Feminism and the LGBTQ movement are under threat, what are we going to do about it?'

Oh God, what was it I read the other day?

Tash: Er... radical self care.

Chloe: Hmm yeah. Read any books lately?

Tash: I'm rereading *Noughts and Crosses*. You?

Chloe: bell hooks, Kimberle Crenshaw, Angela Davis. 'We have to talk about liberating minds as well as liberating society.' They've opened my eyes to a whole new way of seeing the world. Oh my God! This song. I love Janelle Monáe!

Tash: Same!

Chloe: Janelle, Beyonce and Rihanna. The Holy Trinity. Beautiful Black women dominating music. Subverting and reclaiming it for themselves.

Tash: Sure.

I really like Chloe. I feel like she kind of understands me. Rihanna comes on and we head straight to the middle of the dancefloor. We know all the words.

Suddenly blasting out the speakers is 'She take my money!' *('Gold Digger' plays)* 'Gold Digger'! Kanye West! Classic. Everyone shouts 'Ohhh!' and joins us on the dancefloor. Oh no… *(Song stops right before the N word is mentioned)*

Do you all know 'Gold Digger'? How does it go again? The chorus. How does the chorus go? *(Sings with the audience)*

'Now, I ain't sayin' she a gold digger, but she ain't messin' with no broke...' 'But she aint messin' with no broke...'

This club won't sing along. They wouldn't. There's no way this very white queer club advertised as a safe space is going to say the N word... *(Song continues)* Oh, they all do.

I look at Chloe – even she's singing along.

She grabs my arm, leans in and says in an intense way, 'Can I tell you a secret? I've never kissed a Black girl before.'

(Music stops playing.)

Tash: Woah, Chloe. What?

Chloe: Don't look at me like that. I'm just stating facts.

Tash: It's still a weird thing to say.

Chloe: I'm just trying to be flirty. You're acting like I'm a racist. Can't be racist if I'm trying to get with you, can I? Come on, let's dance.

Tash: I need to use the toilet.

(Tash hesitates and then sits on the toilet seat) I know it's gross.

How can you quote Black Feminists and then say that to me? Dancing and singing the N word with joy. Urgh! I should have said... Stupid club! Stupid Chloe! Stupid Kanye! *(Remembers)*

*

Tash: James. I want to be your vice president. Give me those glasses.

James: Oh...? What's changed your mind?

Tash: I've got *a lot* to say.

*

James: *(Blows whistle)* So, campaign strategy! I've divided everyone up into voting blocs, and your key demographics are the gays, the girls and the BAMEs. We'll target them all separately.

Tash: Er, you can't just divide people up like that.

James: Oh, don't be like that. It's politics. Right, there's a Women's Council taking place tonight in the De Beauvoir Lecture Theatre. Now remember what I said. Really milk being a woman. Rock up, give them the old 'men are trash', heteropatriarchal toxic masculinity routine, and they'll be putty in your hands. *(Blows whistle)*

*

Rachel: Hello, sisters. Welcome to the first Women's
　　Council of the academic year. I'm Rachel, Council Chair.

The Women's Council is made up of 6 middle class straight
white cis women who were almost certainly Head Girls at
their private schools.

Rachel: First up on the agenda: abolishing the sexist
　　advertising for Club Nirvana, the campus nightclub.
　　Sarah, could you please present your findings?

Sarah: I am shocked, disgusted and scared. The union thinks
　　it's appropriate to advertise our student nightclub with
　　some of the most vile, degrading images I've ever seen.
　　This week, Freshers are being lured to a so-called 'Vicars
　　& Tarts' themed event, which both degrades women
　　who may be ordained ministers and demeans sex work-
　　ers. It has to be cancelled!

The room cheers.

And then the Council talk for 15 minutes about different
protest tactics. The Secretary suggests a flash mob during
the student rugby finals. 'We'll storm the pitch. Stop the
game. Interruption is the best disruption.' The Finance

19

Officer says, 'Oh, I love a bit of agitprop. Let's make labels that say "#FreeWomen" and stick them over all the posters.' Someone from the crowd shouts out, 'What about a slutwalk?' and the room goes crazy. Now's my chance.

Tash: *(puts hand up)* Hi. I'm Tash, running for Vice President. I think that the posters the student nightclub has put up are disgraceful. I will remove them as soon as I'm elected. I'll make it a priority. A vote for me is a vote to get rid of the evil patriarchy that all women are oppressed by on this campus.

And the room cheers.

Tash: United we stand, divided we fall.

And the rooms cheers some more.

Tash: Men are trash!!

We're whooping, we're clapping, we're stomping and standing on tables. We've become feral.

Tash: Oh, also, The Black Women's Network are launching a campaign around decolonising our curriculums. We

20

should collaborate on raising awareness around the lack of Black women professors at our uni and challenging white hegemony within mainstream feminist discourse.

The room falls silent.

Rachel: Okay. Let's crack on. The second and final item on the agenda: we need the union to build more toilets for women at Club Nirvana. It's unfair that women have to queue for ages to use the toilets. Our bodies and our specific needs aren't being respected!

Voices from the crowd shout 'Yeah!' and 'Respect me!'

Tash: *(Puts hand up)* Absolutely! We also need to make sure the nightclub provides gender neutral toilets as I didn't see any when I was there. And that would help with queues too.

(The room falls silent)

Sisters?

Rachel: This is the *Women's* Council, er – Tash, was it? Gender neutral toilets aren't relevant to the work we're doing.

Tash: Surely this is exactly what the Women's Council should be fighting for? Civil rights? There are students on campus who can't use the nightclub toilets because they're binary and exclusionary. The gender binary harms us all in some way.

Rachel: Oh, right. The LGBTQ Society meets every Thursday on the other side of campus.

Tash: I don't think this is just an LGBTQ issue.

Rachel: *(Irritated)* It is. This has nothing to do with our agenda.

Tash: *(Tash reaches for glasses but stops herself)* I really think we should take a moment to reflect on how to become more representative as a Council. This doesn't feel inclusive.

Rachel: Well, I really think you're starting to dominate the conversation. You're not creating a safe space at all.

Tash: I'm not creating a safe space?

Rachel: You're just starting to sound a little *aggressive* right now...

Tash: Hahaha. *(Tash looks around for support.)* Oh. You mean that? Okay.

Tash puts her glasses on. Everything becomes surreal. Music starts.

Tash: Don't let me get in my zone. Don't let me get in my
   zone. I'm definitely in my zone.

 I don't think you understand who I am.

(She raps)

My name is Tash

That's T-A-S-H

Play nice

And I could be your best mate

Play dumb

And I'm gonna be your biggest hater

Fuck you up

Make you cry, bitch, see you later

Women's Council

But in big big 2020

You got agendas that are

Borderline elementary

Talking 'bout posters

And numbers of toilets

Then you wanna turn around

And act like I spoil it

By speaking up

Wanting things to be more fair

Inclusive. Accessible.

'Tash, don't you dare!'

Calling me aggressive

Like I'm acting wild

I wasn't then

But now you got me really riled

You white girls

Really drive me fucking mad

Where's this sisterhood

That you claim you have?

Council Chair

Coz it's good for your CV

Fuck actual policies

That affect people like me

When I'm VP

This Council's changing quick time

Can't tell me nothing

This whole thing is all mine

Tash takes glasses off.

I've gone viral.

Phone rings.

Tash: Hello?

(To audience) It's Victoria.

(To Victoria) I'm trending on uni Twitter! Uni Twitter. It's like Twitter but uni. Check out #Tash2020.

No, do it now. On the phone. Do it.

Right? Right??

Yeah, yeah, yeah, watch the video.

No, do it now. On the phone. Do it.

Right? Right??

I didn't know I could rap either!

2000 likes.

Vicky, it's these glasses. They're amazing! It's like everything I've wanted to say and more comes out.

What do you mean be careful? I'm viral! Do you know how hard that is for people not just doing their makeup?

Urgh, you don't understand.

Hell no. These are coming with me everywhere.

I've got a campaign to win. Give my love to Aunty Patsy.

*

The Women's Council issue an apology stating that they are going to review their policies and decolonise their agenda, and they're throwing their support behind #Tash2020. I heard members urged Rachel to step down as Chair but she cried so she's still in post.

A card shows up at James's cupboard from the Black Women's Network thanking me for finally calling Rachel's bullshit out.

I AM [NOT] KANYE WEST

The student newspaper, *The Beacon*, writes a feature on me titled 'Our Greatest Hope' which I thought was a bit over the top but... maybe.

I've now been trending on uni Twitter for two days and the video's been seen by 60,000 people.

This is amazing! I'm not sure what's happening but I love it.

*

I've been invited to a spoken word night on campus. Spoken word, rap... I'm sort of in that world now.

The Poetry Society hosts the night in the Ginsberg bar. The place is heaving. I struggle my way to the bar, order a Scrumpy Jack and find a seat.

Then Samuel, head of the unofficial Black Nationalist Society takes to the stage. The union won't recognise the Society after a voice note leaked of a meeting they had where the group discussing Black Power. Caused quite a fright.

27

Samuel:

Black. Dark. Like the other side of the moon.

The side we can't see.

See. See.

Who can I see?

Who sees me?

Me

Everyone starts clicking. So I join in. And a voice next to me says, 'Yo, what the fuck was that?'

Tash: Haha I don't get it either. I thought I was the only one.

Rae: You're not. I'm Rae.

Tash: I'm Tash.

(Tash is instantly enamoured)

Rae is slightly taller than me, has baby locs, sleeve tattoos, real Stud vibes. She's in third year which is *so* hot. She's part of the Black Queer Feminist Forum. And, yeah, I won't lie, I suddenly thought 'shit... I'm going to need to have an *actual* personality now.' I can't just bang on about various forms of oppression. It's not exactly news to her.

We exchange numbers and Whatsapp about *everything*.

She wants to be a documentary filmmaker. I want to be a drama teacher.

She loves anime and I always thought it was called a-nime.

She shares essays by Audre Lorde and James Baldwin and then we have debates, which I now know is definitely my love language. She always wins though. I get too flustered.

She asks me whether I have any childhood emotional wounds that I've carried into adulthood and it catches me off guard. I say, 'I think I only deserve love when I've achieved something.' It was the first time I ever really thought about that.

I ask her and she says, 'I find it hard to assert my boundaries because of my deep fear of abandonment.'

We share secrets. I tell her I think cheese is overrated. She says, 'I'm not really that into Beyonce.'

Tash: Sorry, what?

Rae: She's really talented but I'm just not into that kind of music. I thought we were sharing secrets?

Tash: Not those secrets.

She's perfect! She feels like what home should feel like.

Rae: The Forum's facilitating some community events soon. You should come along.

Tash: I would love to but I've gotta focus on this election. #Tash2020 is still trending and I've got to capitalise.

Rae: Okay. But you know the real power comes from grassroots organising, right? Not being a trend.

Tash: Do you even know what it's like to trend? I've never had that kind of attention before. If this feels good, imagine what winning feels like.

Rae: Just don't get too sucked into the machine. You're only a cog after all.

Tash: James has said at the rate I'm going I might be as influential as him. We'll basically be co-presidents if I win. I'm doing this for us. For representation.

Rae: Alright. I'll text you about these events, yeah? In case you change your mind.

*

I can't wait to tell Victoria about Rae but... It's the first time I've really liked a girl... Which is fine, she's fine about all that. I know that but... Campaign life is just really taking over. I'll call her later.

*

James starts up a #AskTash on uni Twitter.

James: People want to know more about *you*. They love a spectacle. Go wild. Don't forget the glasses.

Twitter: Which historical Black Feminist is your icon?

Tash: I feel I'm too busy writing history to read it.

500 retweets.

Twitter: What's something that really upsets you?

Tash: My greatest pain in life is that I will never be able to see myself perform live.

1000 retweets.

Twitter: Best life advice?

Tash: People always tell you 'Be humble. Be humble.' When was the last time someone told you to be amazing? Be great! Be awesome! Be awesome!

2000 retweets.

Twitter: How do you want to be remembered?

Tash: I will go down as the voice of this generation, of this decade, I will be the loudest voice.

5000 retweets.

*

31

I get sent to the Dean's office after calling my History of Drama lecturer a colonialist in front of everyone.

Dean: You can't just call people colonialists, Natasha.

Tash: Yeah, well he is. Why are all the playwrights on his curriculum white?

Dean: It was a class on Medieval Irish storytelling, Natasha.

Tash: Well... isn't that convenient, Dean.

Dean: You picked the class, Natasha.

Tash: What were my options? Don't you gaslight me!

Around 30 students protest outside in support of me. Hear that? That's the sound of power. Theatre studies must fall!

I can't lie, I'm starting to get a bit nervous. I can't get kicked out of university. My parents will actually kill me. So, you know, I'm obviously going to go back to that class and write my essays. Just don't tell anyone.

*

James tells me that right now I'm the hottest thing on campus.

James: What did I say? People love this shit. The sassy Black girl telling it like it is. Slaying!

Tash: I really don't think I'm saying anything *that* controversial, James.

James: Ha. Epic. Right, Radio Gay are desperate to have you on. It's a good idea. The host, DJ Danny... *(Clears throat)* Fanny, gets a lot of listeners. It'll show you're super-inclusive.

Tash: It's not called Radio Gay. It's called Wilde Waves. You know, after Oscar Wilde. Yet another thing named after a dead white man.

James: Alright, steady on. You're talking to me now, not your fans. Let's not forget the bigger picture. I'm on your side.

Tash: Sorry, yeah.

James: The Vice Presidency is yours for the taking. The other candidates have been completely drowned out. We're going to look really good together.

*

I listen to a few of DJ Danny Fanny's shows for research. Stalk him online. He does have a following. Attractive, slim, white, gay man. I think they're called Twinks. I'm not really familiar with their lingo.

(Radio jingle plays: 'This is DJ Danny Fanny making a fanny of himself every Wednesday on Wilde Waves!')

Danny: So tell me, girlfriend, which member of the Spice Girls do you relate to most?

Tash: What does this have to do with my policies, Danny?

Danny: Just a little bit of fun to warm you up before we talk shop. Are you more Sporty or Baby?

Tash: I've never thought about it.

Danny: They're iconic! Dare I say you're a bit Scary?

Tash: What?

Danny: Well, our listeners know all about you and your antics. Wouldn't want to mess with you!

Tash: It was a white journalist who came up with those names because he couldn't be bothered to learn their actual ones. Baby, Sporty, Posh, Ginger... *Scary*.

Danny: Okay. Let's talk policies, shall we? What are yours?

Tash: Well, listeners, one that is specific to us is I'd like to establish alcohol-free LGBTQ social events on campus, as I think the emphasis on drink within our community can be destructive.

Danny: Sounds a bit... dry. *(laughs)*

Tash: Establishing safe spaces so that all members of the community can take part in social activities is important.

Our community's drinking culture has long excluded LGBTQ Muslims on campus...

Danny: Of course, of course, speak on it! Yaaass kween! She's giving us Policy Realness right now, listeners. Oo, I'm channelling my inner Black woman.

Tash: Some of us have an outer Black woman, Danny.

Danny: For sure, honey. I know our listeners would love the Union to do more to highlight gay men's health. They do enough for the hetties. We don't get any attention.

Tash: Definitely. Especially queer and transgender people of colour.

Danny: I said gay men, Tash. We're really marginalised these days. It's like the G's been pushed to the back of the alphabetti spaghetti, right?

Tash: *(Pulls out glasses, but resists putting them on)* There's more to the community than gay men though.

Danny: Yes, yes, yes, of course, of course. Are you dating? What apps do you lesbians use?

Tash: What's this got to do with anything? I didn't say I was a lesbian, I'm bi... And aren't all those apps weird and racist? 'No Blacks, No Asians', sort of thing?

Danny: Oh for sure. It's terrible but what can we do?

Tash: Not be racist, Danny.

Danny: It's hard for everyone though. I mean, I'm naturally blond and super-slim, so if someone's looking for Idris

Elba, he's not going to be into me, is he? No. This life isn't easy. We've got to pick our battles though, haven't we? Ultimately, we're fighting the same enemy.

Tash: Which is... who?

Danny: Well, where do we start? Wouldn't you say the Black community is still really homophobic?

Tash: Well, we're no more homophobic than the white community.

Danny: I beg to differ but if you say so.

Tash: I do say so. *(Puts shades on)* You know what, Imma let you finish but you're talking a load of shit. I can't believe they got me on this dumb ass radio show debating which community is more homophobic. You gotta come with more than that for your interview, Danny Fanny. Danny *Fanny*? I can't even...

Do you know who I am? Do you know who I am? Have you not seen the shit I do? I'm the number one trend on uni Twitter.

Coz I speak for the left behind. The unheard. The silenced. The forgotten. I don't care about your little white gay cis male problems when you don't care about mine.

We're not fighting the same enemy. You are my enemy. You betray the community and protect the status quo. Get outta here with your 'Yaaass kweens' and your 'inner Black woman'. Who the fuck do you think you are?

Do you know what this election is? No one was talking

about student elections before I came around. Now they got signs everywhere saying #Tash2020. #Tash2020. People are wearing badges! I did that. I'm a genius. I am the champion the people have been waiting for. I don't have to put up with this. I have thousands of people rooting for me. Do you not see my mentions? We're setting this whole thing ablaze. The future is a Black, queer woman. So fuck you, fuck your viewers, fuck your 'queer only means gay white men' and fuck this radio show.

How's that for Scary? Bitch.

*

(Phone rings)

Tash: Not now, Victoria!

Tash paces up and down growing more and more into Kanye.

Tash: If I don't scream, if I don't say something then no one's going to say anything!

Tash: For me to say I wasn't a genius, I would just be lying to you and to myself!

Tash: When you're the absolute best, you get hated on the most!

Tash: Criticism can bother you, but you should be more bothered if there's no criticism. That means you're too safe.

Tash spirals out of control. A mix of Kanye West songs play dysfunctionally, echoing, rewinding, slowing down, speeding up. Kanye's interviews are played. The more outrageous the better. A hellish soundscape. Tash is frenetic. And then everything stops.

*

I haven't eaten a healthy meal in about two weeks. Aunty Patsy would be so mad. I keep ignoring Victoria's calls. Had to ask for an extension on two essays. I haven't made friends with anyone on my course – I think they're scared I'll call them out for liking David Hare. The French Society went to Paris without me. Rae asked me out on a date. She wants to do some volunteering at a food bank but I don't have time for food banks. Or dates. I have an election to win, an identity to defend.

I don't really know or remember what I'm fighting for anymore. I just know that I'm angry all the time and that I absolutely cannot lose this.

*

James: Tash, bad news. The recent polls are out and your approval ratings have really slipped after that radio interview. DJ Danny... has written an op-ed in *The Beacon* labelling you an anti-white militant. Your competitors have tried new tactics – Beth gave a speech about how she's the 'safe choice' for women students, and you're 'problematic'. Ryan's teamed up with the Christian Union. They've released a music video about you titled 'False Prophets'. It's all getting a bit out of hand.

Tash: What are you talking about? You said call things out, make people listen. Everyone loves me. Everyone is here for the revolution.

James: Yes, but there's a line. DJ Danny is very influential. He's telling listeners to vote for fun, not fear. This was your Kanye shoving Taylor Swift off the podium moment. Too far. The mood has shifted and you're becoming a little bit of a problem. Speaking your mind isn't endearing or funny anymore. You're too angry. Don't get me wrong, you're still hugely popular among some crowds, Blacks especially, but don't forget where the majority of votes are coming from. We need to get more people back onside. White people. You've alienated them.

Tash: I was never trying to be funny or endearing. This is my actual life, James. *(Pause)* Maybe I have gotten a bit carried away. How do I stop people feeling alienated?

James: By showing them that you're not actually a threat. People are supportive of your plight, they want a good life for you. You just can't inconvenience them too much. Right, last demographic: the BAMEs. I tried to get the East Asian Student Network and the Black Student Network to host a joint event on your behalf but they weren't having it.

Tash: Because those are separate communities with very different issues.

James: Whatever. The African and Caribbean Society wants you to give a special talk tomorrow night. I agreed. Should be a slam-dunk: these are easy votes. They're a good laugh, always up for a party. The union was concerned by the closed nature of the meeting, though, what with the Black Nationalist anti-white drama, so it's going to be livestreamed into the union bar. Everyone will be watching. Let's try and get people tweeting #Tash2020 again shall we?

*

The next night I arrive at The African and Caribbean Society meeting wishing I knew more people. Thank goodness, straight away I spot Dami.

Dami is the ACS President. Dami is also the best looking guy on campus. He's tall and broad and has the bone structure and shape up of a god. I appreciate him for a little while as he walks up to me.

Tash: Oh, hi, Dami.

Dami: Yo, what you saying, Ms Malcolm X? Glad you could
join us tonight. You know you got my vote. Come here.

He gives me a hug. Dami smells really good because of
course he smells really good.

Victoria would also love Dami.

The room is packed and buzzing and loud. I take my place at
the front, spot James at the back running the livestream. He
gives me a thumbs up.

Tash: Hey, everyone. As most of you know, I'm running for
Vice President. #Tash2020.

They cheer.

Tash: I'm going to platform our issues so that we can finally
be heard on campus.

They cheer some more.

Tash: Black men are constantly being stopped and searched
in the town. Also, Kurtis has told me about the Club

Nirvana incident last week. Shocking that in this day and age a bouncer would say 'we don't let your type in.' Richard has informed me of the high dropout rates for Black men. Adjoa has tried repeatedly to set up an official union investigation into the declining mental health of Black women on campus, to no avail because of indifference from the top. There's a big discrepancy with the distribution of union funds. Why should the Viking Society get more money than us? At every step, we are being disempowered and we can't make progress. This campus is toxic. The discrimination, the isolation, the stereotyping, the gaslighting of our concerns. It's relentless. And it needs to end.

I am sick and tired of it. We need drastic, swift, radical change. Vote for me and I will...

Tash remembers the livestream. Looks at the camera.

Err... look into it. I will take everyone's concerns into consideration, *everyone* on campus, so that we can all reach nice, polite solutions that will bring people together. Vote for Tash, and for unity.

James nods enthusiastically. And then Samuel, from the Black Nationalist Society, stands up and says

Samuel: Nice, polite solutions? Yo, what the fuck is that, fam? You mean to tell me you came here tonight to talk about nice solutions? Where's your rage gone? We're under attack here! It's Black genocide!

Tash: Well, I wouldn't put it like that, Samuel. Steady on. I mean sure, it's all quite overwhelming at the moment. Tensions are high. Everyone's feeling it.

Samuel: Yeah. Are you though?

Tash: I'm absolutely feeling it, Samuel. More than you can imagine, trust me.

Samuel: Swear down? Coz when you first started, when you were speaking for us, I was backing you. I was excited, I thought 'finally'. My girl's telling it like it is. Then you got a bit carried away but whatever, it's calm. It was funny. And, now, overnight, all I've seen are photos of you smiling with the president and posting Insta captions saying 'if we free our minds of victimhood, we can free ourselves.' Must be really *nice* at the top.

Tash: Samuel, I'm running a campaign. It's politics.

Samuel: You know you can't actually change shit. This isn't your game to win.

Tash: You don't know that.

Samuel: You're so naïve. And quick to dash us under the bus too. Makes sense. You got the voice for it. You can't convince me you're from Ends when you talk like that.

Tash: I'm genuinely from Newham.

Samuel: Newham*shire* more like. Right now, you're moving like a opp.

Tash: Well, what would you like me to do?

Samuel: Do something for Black people. That's why we're voting for you, right?

Tash: I'm trying. I've done nothing but stand up for us. Whether it's at the Women's Council or Danny Fanny...

Samuel: Ahhh, nah nah nah don't start that LGB123 bullshit. Don't bring that into this space. The feminism was enough. *(Laughs to his friend)* Spud me, spud me. *(Back to Tash)* I don't care about no gay shit. Or what is it, 'queer'? That's white people shit. Who cares what you're doing for them? In this room, we're pro-Black. Black comes first. Before everything. What are you doing for us?

Long pause as Tash looks around the room for support but receives none.

Tash: I am 'us', Samuel. *(Looks into the camera)* I am us, Rachel. I am us, Danny. I am Black, a woman, working class, queer. Together. At the same time. It can't be divided up. James, it can't be divided up.

I am so tired.

'Call things out, Tash, but not too much!', 'Toe the line, Tash, but now you're a sell out.' Do you know what? Fuck this! I can't rationalise the irrational.

You don't give a fuck about gay shit, Samuel? You don't give a fuck about feminism? Great. I don't give a fuck about your male anxieties. I don't give a fuck about no Black man who disregards my life, my needs, my liberation but expects me to back him when the time comes. So fuck you, Samuel.

Tash looks at the glasses, realises she's said this without them on.

And fuck you, Kanye. You are a rich, entitled, privileged man. We are not the same. You don't care about me.

Tash throws the glasses stage left.

None of you do. You're all too concerned with flexing the tiny bit of power you have over me. I just wanted some for myself. But it's impossible. This livestream watching me, watching us fight amongst ourselves. On social media, on radio stations, in the press. Coz it's entertaining, coz it's a distraction. And, after we've torn each other apart, who wins?

*

Not me. I didn't win. James is President and Beth is his VP.

*

James: It's been a crazy ride, Tash. It would have been good to have you on my team but you know how these things go. It's politics. Beth was always my second preference anyway. I would've offered you Diversity Officer but we don't have the budget for one anymore… I heard everyone cancelled you. Hey, you know that doesn't really mean much in the long run. Look after yourself though. Maybe go and see the student counsellor or something.

Tash: James. Go fuck yourself.

*

(Deep breath) Well, that's one way to start uni. I cannot believe I have to be here for three years.

Don't tell my family about this. It's bad enough facing Victoria.

Victoria: Fam, I could have told you from time that white men ain't shit. You played yourself.

Tash: I'm gutted. He promised me gold, Victoria. And, like a fool, I fell for it.

Victoria: Yes, you did. Mediocre white men. They got the system on lock. What? Don't look at me like that. I might not know all the big words you use, but I do know a thing or two about how the world works. And I'm always willing to learn more.

Tash: I'm sorry, Vix.

Victoria: It's alright. But don't ever ignore my calls again. It was jokes, though. You said you were the voice of a generation.

It's the Christmas holidays. I'm in my Aunty Patsy's hair salon. My best friend, Victoria, is doing my hair. Everyone is here. Aunties who aren't my aunties, cousins I didn't know I had, the next door neighbour, the Chinese manicurists, the Yardie I can't understand. The place smells like Morley's. A game show is muted on the TV. Vybz Kartel's homophobic lyrics are on the radio. Everything is how everything is.

Aunty Patsy: Ey, lesbian boots. How you been? Me nah see nuttin on Facebook fe time.

Tash: I don't really use social media that much, Aunty, it's too distracting. But, yeah, great. Nothing to report.

Victoria: So who's this hot girl you wanted to tell me about?

Tash: Oh, Rae. Yeah. I nearly messed that up. Luckily, she's got a thing for headstrong, passionate girls. We've been

Whatsapping. About killing capitalism. We've decided to go straight to the source.

Victoria: Jesus. I thought you were over all of this.

Tash: Over? Victoria, I'm sad but I'm not dead. No, I'm only just getting started. *(To the audience)* Next term. New tactics.

End

Also available from Team Angelica Publishing

Prose

'Reasons to Live' by Rikki Beadle-Blair
'What I Learned Today' by Rikki Beadle-Blair
'Faggamuffin' by John R Gordon
'Colour Scheme' by John R Gordon
'Souljah' by John R Gordon
'Drapetomania' by John R Gordon
'Fairytales for Lost Children' by Diriye Osman
'Cuentos Para Niños Perdidos' – Spanish language edition,
    trans. Héctor F. Santiago
'Black & Gay in the UK' ed. John R Gordon & Rikki
    Beadle-Blair
'Sista! – an anthology' ed. Phyll Opoku-Gyimah,
    John R Gordon & Rikki Beadle-Blair
'More Than – the Person Behind the Label' ed. Gemma Van
    Praagh
'Tiny Pieces of Skull' by Roz Kaveney
'Fimí sílè Forever' by Nnanna Ikpo
'Lives of Great Men' by Chike Frankie Edozien
'Lord of the Senses' by Vikram Kolmannskog

Playtexts

'Slap' by Alexis Gregory
'Custody' by Tom Wainwright
'#Hashtag Lightie' by Lynette Linton
'Summer in London' by Rikki Beadle-Blair